What Would Dad Do?

by
Paul T. Morgan

© 2021 Paul T. Morgan

All rights reserved. No part of this book may be reproduced or transmitted in any form or by any means whatsoever without express written permission from the author. The scanning, uploading and distribution of this book via the Internet or via any other means without the permission of the author is illegal and punishable by law. For permission requests, contact the author at the email address: pmorgan817@yahoo.com.

ISBN paperback: 978-1-7369886-1-9
ISBN ebook: 978-1-7369886-0-2

Cover and Text Design: Rick Soldin

Printed in the United States of America

My sincere gratitude to my children Reagan and Meredith for the inspiration to write this book, and to my wife Elaine for the encouragement to get it published

—Paul

Contents

Your Personal Values 1

Your Relationship with Others 47

That's Life 79

How Our World Works 85

Wrap-up 99

Preface

It is a centuries-old tradition within the Jewish faith for parents to write and deliver to their children an "ethical will"—a document that passes down a set of personal values and counsel from one generation to the next. I stumbled across an online book a few years ago that encouraged modern-day parents to do the same for their children as a way to help them understand the values and principles that shaped the way they were raised. I loved the idea—especially in light of our family's life circumstances.

My late wife Jan was diagnosed with early-onset Alzheimer's Disease at age 49. Our son Reagan and daughter Meredith were teenagers at the time. If you know anything about Alzheimer's Disease and how quickly it robs its victims of their cognitive faculties, you have a picture of how that diagnosis changed our family's world. At way-too-early ages, Reagan and Meredith had to step up and tag-team with Dad as family caregivers for their Mom. That life-changing experience both reinforced so many of the life lessons we had already been teaching them and introduced some new ones that more fairly should have waited a few years.

Every dad, of course, believes his own kids are the greatest. Mine are. You can't imagine how compassionately and selflessly they helped me care for their Mom. They didn't "need" me to write this letter to make good choices in life.

But watching Jan pass away at a relatively young age impressed upon me the fragility of life—the fact that none of us is promised a life into our golden years. And if there is anything you want to say to someone, don't assume that you have forever to say it.

The following letter to Reagan and Meredith was simply my effort to share with them again many of the life lessons they had been hearing from Mom and Dad all their lives along with a few topics we just never got around to discussing. So I sent this letter to them as a reverse Father's Day gift three years ago. It was never my intention to publish the letter for others to read.

So why now publish a very personal letter to my kids? I saw how graciously my kids received this gift from their Dad. And I think other adult children would benefit from receiving a similar letter from their parents. So I decided to publish my letter in book form as my challenge to other parents to write their own ethical will letters to their kids.

I include my own values here NOT because I think other parents should embrace the same values (although some of them are pretty universal) but just to provide a template of the kinds of life situations and values parents should be discussing with their kids. If you accept my challenge to write a similar letter to your own kids, choose the topics and values that are meaningful to you. But feel free to also borrow any of what I've included here—heck, most of them I borrowed from somebody else anyway.

I hope you enjoy reading my letter. But more than that, I hope it inspires you to pick up your own pen (or keyboard) and give your own children the gift of knowing in certain situations what their dad (or mom) would do.

Paul T. Morgan

What Would Dad Do?

Dear Reagan and Meredith:

Most older adults spend a great deal of time preparing for the financial and legal aspects of their lives. They prepare a will that stipulates what possessions will be passed down to whom when they die. This is all about trying to direct the influence we'll have on our families when we are no longer around to direct those influences. But I read a book a while back that suggested that more important than the **financial legacy** we pass down to our children is the **value legacy** we pass on to them. What values and life lessons will they "inherit" from us that might somehow make their own lives richer?

All my life I've heard people say something like, "Like my daddy used to say…" or "My mom always told me to…" So, I began to wonder: what advice or life lessons will the two of you recall from me? Have I done everything I can to help you develop the value system that will guide your own lives?

So, a few years ago I began writing this "letter" for the two of you—a combination of advice and personal value statements. Some of the thoughts are original but most of them are ideas or values I've borrowed from other people over time. The idea here is NOT to try to tell you what to believe or to suggest that you embrace the same values and priorities that I hold. It's simply to share some observations and experiences from having now lived 60+ years and give you some food for thought as you develop your own values and priorities.

I'm hoping you won't read this once and file it away for my obituary someday, but that you'll go back and read it over from time to time as a reminder of the values that shaped the way Mom and I raised you. Embrace the values that make sense to you, and discard the ones that don't. But in either case, if you ever wonder, "What would Dad do?"—well, now you know.

Love,
Dad

Chapter One
Your Personal Values

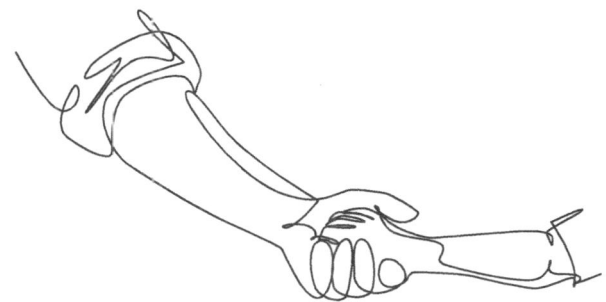

Self-restraint

There's a really cute video on YouTube that shows young kids being filmed in a test of their self-restraint. In the test, the kids are placed in a room alone with a large marshmallow on a plate in front of them. The teacher tells them she is going to leave the room for just five minutes. She tells each child that he has two choices while she's gone: he can either eat the marshmallow now, or if he waits until she returns, he can have *two* marshmallows and eat them both. The teacher then leaves the room, leaving the kids alone with their marshmallows—and their difficult choice. The expressions on their faces during the eternity of those five minutes are priceless as each child weighs the options of something really good now vs. something even better if they wait.

Self-restraint is far superior to self-indulgence. Our society has a mindset of "instant gratification"—wanting to have everything *now*. This impatience causes people to make poor choices, frequently giving up a lot of happiness or security in the future in order to have some of it now. This is what causes people to go into debt or make impulsive purchases that they later regret or for which they cannot pay.

If something is worth having, it's probably worth waiting for. And frequently, the "wait" can actually make it more gratifying when you get it. Or sometimes, waiting allows time for a more rational assessment of the decision and can save you from making a poor choice.

Arrogance

A battleship was at sea in foggy weather. One night, the lookout on the bridge suddenly shouted, "Captain! A light, bearing on the starboard bow." The captain asked, "Is it stationary or moving astern?" The lookout replied that it was stationary.

Fearing a head-on collision, the captain immediately ordered his signalman to send out a signal: "We are on a collision course. I advise you to change course 20 degrees east." Back came a signaled response, "You should change your course 20 degrees west." Agitated by the non-compliant response, the captain asked his signalman to shoot out another message: "I am a captain, you change course 20 degrees east." Back came the second response: "I am a second class seaman, change your course 20 degrees west."

The captain was furious now. He shouted to the signalman to send back a final message: "I am a battleship. Change course 20 degrees east NOW!" Back came the flashing response: "I am a lighthouse. Change your course 20 degrees west."

There are few personality traits that will turn people off quicker than arrogance. But beyond its off-putting effect on others, it is also a trait that can lead one to ignore very sound advice and make very poor decisions.

Paul T. Morgan

Ethical Behavior

My favorite definition of ethical behavior is doing the right thing when no one is watching. The story is told (apparently true) about a successful and rising member of his company's management team who was chosen for promotion to vice-president. He was invited to the company's cafeteria to eat a celebratory lunch with other officers. While going through the serving line, he slid a two-cent pat of butter under his dinner roll so it would not be visible to the cashier. He then paid for his lunch without revealing the hidden butter pat. The company's CEO was in line behind him, witnessed the whole incident and fired the new VP before he could even assume his new position—telling the board that if the man would be dishonest in small things, you can bet he'll someday be dishonest in larger things. I side with the CEO in that judgment.

Honesty and Integrity— the "Gray" Areas

Most honesty and integrity questions are easily answered: the "right" answer to a moral dilemma is often obvious (e.g. don't lie, don't steal, etc.). But life will frequently deal you some situations where the moral choice is not so black and white. So how do you decide what's right in these "gray" areas? I like the advice Warren Buffet gives his business managers for making these choices: "Imagine that your actions will be reported on the front page of your local newspaper by a fair but critical reporter who has knowledge of all the facts." If you're comfortable knowing that all your friends and family will read about your intended actions in the newspaper, you're probably making a good choice. If not …

Paul T. Morgan

Reputation

Your words and actions will affect your reputation. That's pretty obvious. But what's not as obvious is how your words and actions can affect the reputation of those close to you: other family members, friends, your employer, your church. None of us is an island. You owe it to yourself to conduct yourself in a manner that is honorable. You have the same obligation to those close to you. It takes a long time to build a good reputation. It can take even longer to *re-build* it.

Be the Person Your Dog Thinks You Are

(This one should be self-explanatory)

Paul T. Morgan

Work Ethic

A strong work ethic will serve you well throughout your working career. You'll be surprised how much your professional success will be affected by the little things you do vs. how smart or talented you are. So, what makes a work ethic strong? Give your employer (or customer) a little bit more than he expects. Show up a bit earlier than you're asked to arrive and don't be in a hurry to leave at "quitting time." Complete your assigned tasks ahead of time, not at the last minute. Be willing to do the "dirty jobs" that everyone else seems to avoid. Be innovative and creative. Be a self-starter.

One of my favorite illustrations of this message was Meredith's job interview for the admissions counselor position at ACU. All she was asked to do (and all that was expected of her) was to present a stock PowerPoint slide deck prepared by the admissions department as a prop for candidates to demonstrate their presentation skills. But on less than a day's notice to prepare, she filmed and edited a video, interviewing students about what they liked about ACU—and then integrated her video into the stock slide presentation. The admissions staff was blown away by the self-starting initiative and creativity she put into her presentation (I know this because more than one of them called me personally to tell me so!). It was the perfect example of my point here: under-promise and over-deliver.

Reliability / Dependability

Whether in your occupation, volunteer service or just in your relationship with friends and family, build a reputation for being someone who can be counted on—do what you say you'll do, be where you're supposed to be and be there on time.

Paul T. Morgan

Personal Accountability

Don't play the victim card. Decisions have consequences. When you make a poor decision and the consequences are bad, own up to it and deal with it. Don't blame your circumstances on someone else and don't expect someone else (or the government) to fix your problems. You've heard it forever: you can't always control your circumstances, but you can control how you respond to them. Or as one of my golf buddies likes to say, "It's a poor workman who blames his tools."

Can You Sleep When the Wind Blows?

Two young men replied to a help-wanted ad from the local yacht club. The posted job was for someone to look after the boats in the harbor and secure them away at night. One of the two applicants touted his experience working with boats and impressed the yacht club owner with his knowledge of boating jargon. The other applicant admitted that he'd never worked on a boat before but told the owner, "I can sleep when the wind blows." The owner wasn't sure what he meant by that comment, but hired both of the young men anyway, assigning each of them to watch over half the boats in the harbor fleet.

A few nights later, a strong storm hit the harbor at midnight. The next morning, the yacht club owner found all the boats safe and secure. He asked the new workers what they had done when the storm hit last night. The more experienced of the two young workers proudly proclaimed that he sprang from his bed and raced down to the harbor in the storm to make sure all the boats under his watch were tied down and secured. The other young man (knowing he had done his job properly before leaving that day) said he simply rolled over and went back to sleep. Only then did the yacht club owner understand what the young man meant by saying that he could sleep when the wind blows.

The lesson here: always handle your responsibilities well and you won't have to panic "when the wind blows."

Paul T. Morgan

Look Around—You Can Always Find Someone Worse Off Than You Are

In a perfect world (and by the way, there isn't one) you would never encounter hard times—life would forever be nothing but rainbows and unicorns. Spoiler alert—not gonna be that way.

There's a parable about a small village of people who were so unhappy - each of them convinced that their own plight in life was worse than they deserved and far worse, they assumed, than any of their fellow citizens. Tired of their grumbling, one day God sent an angel to town to announce that everyone in town would be given the opportunity to exchange his troubles for those of a fellow townsman. The angel instructed them, "Pack all your troubles in a bag and leave your bag at the courthouse tonight. Tomorrow morning, you may then select any bag you choose for yourself." A mad chase ensued the next morning with everyone scrambling to get back his own bag.

You may sometimes think your own troubles are big and unfair. But look around—you can always find someone else worse off than you are.

Faith

It is common for people to "inherit" the faith of their parents. Most people wind up adopting a faith that is the same as (or very similar to) the one in which they grew up. But you need to develop your own personal faith. And it might or might not look exactly like the one in which Mom and I raised you.

There are hundreds of religious faiths in the world and dozens of variations and differences of opinion among the people within each of them. There's no way to "prove" whose faith is right or wrong. If it could be proved, everyone would believe the same thing.

From my perspective, the evidence for "intelligent design" is overwhelming. I don't see how anyone could look at the complexity of our world and argue that it simply "just happened." But who or what intelligent designer was behind it all? That's where all the different faiths come in.

The Bible is just one of many versions of the intelligent design theory. It's the version that our family has embraced for many generations, and its version makes more sense to me than any of the others. But frankly, there are lots of pieces of the Bible's story that are hard for me to accept or understand. There are some statements in the Bible that seem to me to be inconsistent with what science and history tell us. I know people who swear that they "know" the Bible's story is true and they have absolutely no questions about it. I wish I could tell you that I have that same confidence. But I don't. I have lots of questions about the Bible for which I doubt I'll ever find the answers. That's why they call it "faith" instead of "knowledge."

So, here's what I think about faith: No matter how hard you try, you're never going to find all the answers. At some point, you have to accept the version of the faith story that makes the most sense to you, and then choose to live by that version. I guess that's what they call the "leap of faith." Live by the principles and guidelines of that faith, and don't get hung up on all the pieces of it that you can't explain or validate.

Don't Let Anyone Else Own Your Happiness

One definition of self-esteem is a confidence in one's own worth or abilities. When others praise you, it boosts your self-esteem. When others criticize you, it deflates your self-esteem. But if what someone else thinks of you is that important, is it really *self*-esteem?

Self-esteem is very important to one's happiness. And it's natural to allow what others think of you to affect what you think of yourself. It's tempting to rely too heavily on the validation you receive when others think highly of you—and to get depressed when they hold the opposite opinion of you. But it shouldn't be that way.

Make sure only your *self* is in charge of your *self*-esteem. And don't let anyone else own your happiness.

Paul T. Morgan

Don't Give Too Much Weight to What the "Experts" Think

You will be constantly surrounded by (sometimes well-intentioned) people in "official roles" who hold very strong opinions—and feel that it is their "duty" to influence you to hold the same views. Because they hold official positions of power, teachers, politicians, preachers and the talking heads on television may try to convince you that they are smarter, better-informed or more intuitive than you are—and so, their positions on issues should carry extra weight when choosing for yourself what views to hold.

Certainly, the truly objective insight of educated and experienced "experts" should be respected. We should give an extra measure of weight to a doctor's opinion on medical treatments or a scientist's recommendations on how to address the risks of a pandemic. But when it comes to matters of opinion, your faith, political views or social issues, your views are just as important as theirs. Listen to informed opinions, but never let someone else (including me!) tell you what to think.

If It Sounds Too Good to Be True

You will encounter lots of "opportunities" in life to buy into something where the benefits appear far superior to the cost. Most things in life are fairly priced based upon the true value of the product or service. There hasn't been a free lunch since God sent the manna and quail. So, if a deal seems too good to be true, it probably isn't true. Caveat emptor (let the buyer beware).

Paul T. Morgan

Once You Make Your Purchase, Quit Shopping

Everyone likes to think they got "a good deal" when they make a significant purchase—a new car, a vacation package, a new set of golf clubs, whatever. And for some reason, frequently they derive as much joy and satisfaction from getting the good deal as they do from the thing itself. So much so, that even after making the purchase, they will continue to check the price of whatever they bought—hoping, I guess, that they will find that the price is even higher now, validating that they did indeed negotiate a good deal. Okay but what if they then find a lesser price after their purchase? Now a purchase about which they were once so excited brings them buyer's remorse.

Once you make your purchase, you're done—quit shopping!

Comparison Is the Thief of Joy

The title of this section is a quote from President Theodore Roosevelt. So true. To compare yourself to others who have more, who have done more, who know more (or in any other way can "more" you) will only cheapen what you think of your own possessions or accomplishments. What someone else has achieved or gained (through circumstances or challenges different from yours) is an irrelevant measuring stick for your own achievements. Don't fall for the trap of comparison to others—and don't let anyone else make those comparisons for you either.

Paul T. Morgan

Learn From Your Mistakes

My ultimate wish for you is that you would never encounter hardship or unhappiness and that you'll never make any mistakes. Not going to happen. You *will* make mistakes in life. When you do, it's okay to be regretful, but don't beat yourself up so badly that you can't move on. Learn from your mistakes and just try not to make the same mistake over and over. As Will Rogers said, "Good judgment comes from experience. And a lot of that experience comes from bad judgment."

Don't Follow a Bad Decision With a Worse One

In the 1999 Open Championship at the famed Carnoustie Golf Club, French golfer Jean Van de Velde stood on the tee of the final hole with a three-shot lead. Three shots clear of his closest competitor, and playing a difficult driving hole, TV commentators were certain Van de Velde would "play it safe"—lay up short of the trouble spots, take an easy bogey (or even double bogey) and hoist the claret jug as champion. But the Frenchman didn't want to lamely "back into" the championship, so he took driver and took on the difficult shot. As the TV analysts looked on in disbelief, Van de Velde pushed his tee shot way right. But his ball stopped short of the water that would have cost him a penalty stroke—Lady Luck saved him from his poor decision. From there he could still play safely, take his medicine and win. But noooooooo.

Undeterred by his bad shot, he tried an even riskier shot over another water hazard. That shot also flew wayward, hitting a grandstand railing and caroming into tall grass. It was a tough lie in the tall grass, but he only needed to make a double bogey to win. Play safely to the back of the green, take your six and claim the championship. Nope.

He attempted the "hero shot" from the grass and hit the ball into the water. Fast forward to the end—Van de Velde makes a triple bogey seven and then loses to Paul Lawrie in a play-off.

Paul T. Morgan

You will make some bad decisions. Lots of them. But when you do, slow down your thinking, take your medicine and find the best way out of trouble from there. Don't let pride cause you to follow a bad decision with a worse one.

Laugh

A lot.

Paul T. Morgan

Never Try to Make a Happy Baby Happier

Just another version of the old "If it ain't broke, don't fix it" proverb. It's trite and overused but there really is a lot of wisdom in this idea: if something is going well, leave it alone—you might make things worse.

You Can Do More Than You Think You Can

Imagine how poorly trained Harriet Tubman was for what became the most important job of her life. How could being raised as a slave with no education have prepared Harriet for leading fellow slaves through their dangerous journeys to freedom? If she had stopped to wonder "Can I do this?" she might never have even started. But her passion and determination overcame whatever physical or educational barriers she faced.

If you had asked me 20 years ago whether I could serve as a family caregiver and perform all the unpleasant hands-on tasks that go with providing in-home personal care to a dementia patient, I'd have said, "No way." I had no training in personal care and quite frankly, some of those tasks are simply disgusting. But when Mom got sick and duty called, I found I could learn to do some things that I didn't really want or know how to do. The lesson here: when duty calls (especially for someone you love) there are few limits to what you can do when you have to.

Paul T. Morgan

Aim Small, Miss Small

Some of the best golf instructors use this advice to get their players laser-focused on their target: not just a tree - a specific branch on the tree, not just the hole - the left-center part of it. The idea of this teaching is that if you focus very narrowly on a small and specific target, even if you miss it by a little bit, you'll be close—a narrow target will yield a narrow miss. Your miss on a broader target will be much broader.

It won't take a lot of imagination to find applications of this golf strategy to lots of areas of your life.

Heroes and Role Models

Heroes are people we don't know but whose achievements inspire us to dream big for our own achievements: sports figures, astronauts, world leaders. We may or may not admire their character—and we may or may not choose to be like them. But they make us say, "Wow!"

Role models are people we know pretty well. They may or may not be well-known or have achieved great things in life. But we know their character, how they live their lives, how they treat other people. They also make us say, "Wow!" - but for different reasons. We want to be like them.

Heroes are for *inspiration*. Role models are for *imitation*. Don't get the two mixed up.

Paul T. Morgan

What Me Worry?

There is nothing that can rob the joy from your life like a steady diet of worrying.

When I was a kid, there was a goofy (but very popular) satire magazine called *Mad*. Its central figure was a cartoonish boy named Alfred E. Neuman: his life motto—what me worry? Alfred was the patron saint of aloofness.

But Alfred wasn't the only influencer to address this problem. Jesus spent a great deal of his teaching on the joy-robbing subject of worrying. Paraphrasing his lesson in Matthew Chapter 6: "If God will take care of the lilies who neither work nor make their own clothes, would he not take care of us, too?"

As is true for most pieces of counsel, there are extremes to be avoided. Jesus was not advocating Alfred E. Neuman's carefree, reckless and irresponsible glide through life. Rather, I think, he was asking us to not be distracted (and dispirited) by imagining every possible thing that could go wrong.

A more modern version of this teaching is the Serenity Prayer: *God grant me the serenity to accept the things I cannot change, the courage to change the things I can, and the wisdom to know the difference.*

Great advice here. Don't waste time, energy or emotion worrying about a situation that is beyond your control.

Get Your News from More Than One Source

Fans are filing out of the stadium after the annual Texas-OU football game. As they walk to their cars, a rabid stray dog attacks a small child in the group. A fan, dressed from head to toe in OU colors, quickly jumps on the dog, pulls it away from the child, and kills it barehanded.

In the crowd, witnessing the whole scene, are the editors of the school papers from both Texas and OU. Both school papers carry the story on the front page of their respective editions the following week, but under very different story titles:

OU Daily: *Courageous Sooner Fan Saves Small Child from Certain Death*

The Daily Texan: *Hillbilly Redneck Murders Beloved Family Pet*

When I was growing up, there were very few sources for news: only three television channels and a single local newspaper. And because both television networks and newspapers depended heavily upon reporting from pools like the Associated Press or UPI, you got pretty much the same storyline no matter which source you used.

But today there are hundreds of news outlets and social media platforms all competing for viewers and readers. Their owners

Paul T. Morgan

and editors must wrestle with their competitors for market share. And they've learned that the best way to carve out a market niche for themselves is to target a specific demographic audience and report the news (i.e. spin it) to the delight of that specific demographic.

Watch both CNN and Fox News report on any given story from the day and you'll wonder if they are describing the same event. One spins the story with a decidedly left slant while the other spins it to the right. Maybe it was always this way and I was just too naïve to notice, but news sources are no longer simply trying to inform—they seek to entertain and influence. And if you consistently rely upon any single news source for your information about politics, business, social issues, etc. you're unlikely to see the full unfiltered story.

Want to stay informed but be allowed to form your own opinions on issues of the day? Select multiple (and divergent) sources for your news.

"You Can Do ANYTHING You Put Your Mind to" … Well, Maybe

I can't count how many times I've watched an interview with the winner of a sporting event and heard him or her say something like, "My mom always told me that I could do *anything* if I put my mind to it. This win proves she was right." So, what about the guys in the other locker room whose moms told them the same thing?

I get the point: it's good to have dreams and be willing to work hard toward achieving them. And sometimes that hard work will be rewarded with that achievement. But some people have big dreams, work hard, do everything within their power to get there … and still come up short. That doesn't mean they were failures.

I would never discourage you from dreaming big and working to realize those dreams. Just the opposite—I hope you *do* dream big and work to achieve whatever you dream. But I'm not going to promise you that every dream will be realized. Sometimes dreams and goals need to be adjusted as our circumstances in life change. Don't be afraid to dream. But don't be afraid to adjust your dreams when appropriate.

Paul T. Morgan

Doing Nothing is a Strategy

When facing a tough situation, it is natural to assume that action is required - and the more dire the situation, the more immediate the action. Your mind tells you, "Don't just sit there—DO something!" And most often there is a something that should be done. But not always.

Doing nothing is a strategy. Sometimes the situation will resolve itself. Sometimes waiting to respond will buy time for better options to appear. And sometimes showing patience will cause your adversary to "blink first" and change his position.

One of my bosses early in my career was a master at the negotiating art of saying nothing. He knew that silence was deafening during a heated negotiation and that frequently the other party would grow impatient for a resolution and offer a bit more than he intended. A calm, quiet, peaceful visage will simply drive a boisterous, agitated adversary nuts.

Never Try to Teach a Pig to Sing

Never try to teach a pig to sing—you won't be successful, and you'll annoy the pig.

Warren Buffet asks all his managers to keep their businesses focused on what he calls their core competencies. That's his way of saying, "Do what you do well and don't get distracted into wandering off into areas that are outside your area of knowledge or expertise." (E.g. If you're in the brick business, don't go open up a grocery store).

Two divergent thoughts here: (1) If you never try anything new, you'll never develop any new competencies, but (2) It's okay to admit that something is beyond your expertise and hire someone to do it for you. Both points have merit. The trick is knowing when to apply each of them. That discernment could have saved me a $400 garage door repair one night ☹

Paul T. Morgan

Pollyanna and Chief Dark Cloud

Some people who have known me a long time (outside a business setting) have frequently called my Pollyanna, referencing the blindly optimistic movie character who always found the good side of any person she encountered. Maybe that's because I like to imagine that, until they prove to me otherwise, everyone I know is deep down a good person. If a driver cuts me off on the freeway, well, he probably had a bran muffin for breakfast and needs to find an off-ramp to a bathroom fast.

But during my career as a chief financial officer, it was frequently my role to play the devil's advocate during meetings—making sure the group had considered "everything that could go wrong" with any project or major decision being contemplated. I wasn't necessarily trying to talk them out of the idea—just ensuring that important decisions were made with their eyes wide open. But my penchant for pointing out the cloud behind the silver lining earned me the good-natured moniker of Chief Dark Cloud among my officer peers.

Split personality? No, I just think it's possible to carry a cautious and healthy skepticism without imagining the worst in people or situations.

Take Care of Your Health

It's easy to fall into the trap of believing your happiness later in life will be primarily determined by your standard of living—how much money you make and the things in life that money can buy. But as I've grown older, I've watched so many friends and family members (some of whom who have enjoyed great financial success) have their enjoyment of life robbed by poor health that prevented them from doing the things their money could have otherwise allowed them to do. You don't have to be a fanatic about exercise or eating right, but practice moderation in your diet, watch your weight and stay physically active throughout your life. The older I get, the better I understand that happiness depends more upon your *health* than your *wealth* (although a combination of both is best!).

Paul T. Morgan

Mentoring

Find a mentor. Be a mentor. We'd all like to think that we are solely responsible for whatever successes we achieve. And sometimes that will be true. But more often, what we achieve in life will come with a little aid from someone else who took a special interest in us, gave us some good advice or helped introduce us to the opportunity on which we capitalized. Find older people in your lives who seem to you to be wise, principled and successful people. Seek their advice. Ask what they would do if faced with whatever difficulty you're facing. And then as you grow older, do the same for the younger people in your lives. You know, the whole "pay it forward" thing.

And by the way, there is a difference between a mentor and a role model. Usually, a role model never knows the people who might be looking at him or her with admiration and imitation. It's a very unintentional influence. A mentoring relationship is very intentional - a mutual bond of friendship and trust to which both parties have agreed to take part.

Not Everything You Have the Right To Do Is a Good Idea

Our nation was founded on the principle of individual rights—a principle that has served us well and protected us from what could otherwise have been an overbearing central government. But what serves us well can sometimes serve us poorly. We frequently hear people defend their selfish actions by proclaiming that they have the "right" to do whatever it was they said or did—as if having the right to do something is the only criterion by which to judge whether a decision was wise. From a purely legal perspective, we probably have the right to be mean, hurtful, selfish and stupid. But frequently you (and those around you) are better served when you choose *what's right to do* over *what you have the right to do*. Not everything you have the right to do is a good idea.

Paul T. Morgan

Risk Tolerance

Life will present lots of risk / reward situations: an opportunity for a big upside reward that carries with it the possibility of a huge loss if things go badly. Examples: business investments, job opportunities, family decisions, etc. Some people thrive on taking big chances. Life is not interesting for them unless they are chasing the big dream. And they're okay if things turn out badly—they had to try it anyway. I'm not cut out that way. I've always been very risk adverse. The downside result of a risky decision that goes badly will stay with me a long time.

Choosing one's risk tolerance level is a very personal choice. The "right" answer for you will not always be obvious. And the right choice for me might not make sense for you. So, here's the test: Ask yourself if you can live with the downside if things go badly. If the answer is "yes" then go for it—and then be willing to accept the consequences if you don't get the outcome for which you hoped. But if the answer is "no" it's time to pass on it. The disappointment of a missed opportunity will not sting nearly as long as the guilt of a risky choice that goes badly.

Live Within Your Means

Ideally, you'll earn lots of money and be able to afford everything you want and need in life. More likely, you'll earn enough to live comfortably but not enough to be able to purchase *everything* you'd like to have. It's also likely that you'll have friends who have more "stuff" than you do and you'll be tempted to live beyond your means (i.e. borrow money) in order to have the same things yourself. Resist that temptation.

When you borrow money to purchase something today, you're sacrificing something in the future - something you may want or need even more. You can spend a dollar on anything you want, but you can only spend it once (translation—every dollar you spend is a dollar *not* available to spend on anything else).

Before making a significant expenditure, apply the "value proposition" test: "Would I rather have this item now, a different item now that costs the same amount or keep my powder dry and wait for something later that I may want even more?"

Purchase a modest home. Drive a reasonably priced car. Spend modestly on recreation and entertainment. Do this and you'll probably find that you can afford to occasionally "splurge" for something special.

Paul T. Morgan

Borrowing Money

Following up the message in the preceding section ...

The ultimate definition of living within your means would be to *never* borrow money for *anything*. Unfortunately, there are a few things in life that are simply too expensive to purchase all at once. But only a few things.

My general rules of thumb for borrowing money are: (1) It should be something you need, and (2) It should be something that will last longer than the time you spend repaying the loan. Houses and cars meet these tests. College for your children also meets these tests because I think the value lasts for a lifetime (although it's possible to save much of the cost of your children's college during their childhood days if you start early enough). Living expenses, vacations and entertainment do *not* meet these tests.

Most people who get into trouble borrowing money don't get there buying cars or houses. They borrow by using their credit cards to finance living expenses or entertainment. Credit cards are a convenient way to make purchases and most cards carry some rebates or rewards that actually pay you for using them—but only if you can pay off the full balance every month. This is probably the best test of living within your means: Can you pay all your bills as they come due and carry no balances on your credit cards?

Money Can't Buy Happiness But ...

There are so many proverbs about money. It can't buy happiness. It's the root of all evil. It's difficult for a rich person to go to heaven.

Certainly, money (or more precisely, the pursuit of it) can wreck marriages, friendships and personal lives. In the 1987 movie *Wall Street*, central character Gordon Gekko proudly proclaims that "greed is good." It's not. But for all its potential for harm, money can in fact make your life better.

Too much money can indeed bring trouble. Look how many lottery winners end up with ruined lives. But too little of it can also bring plenty of pain. People who lack the financial resources to be self-supporting are treated very harshly in America. Probably shouldn't be that way, but it is. Having "enough" money can ward off a lot of problems. People with financial wherewithal don't have to forego medical treatments they can't afford or live in squalid conditions or never take family vacations or work until they die because they can't afford to retire.

Two points here: Never make the pursuit of money become so important that it upsets your priorities, but don't be afraid to work hard, seek out ways to earn more money (the right way!) and put yourself in a financial position that can protect you from some of life's calamities.

Paul T. Morgan

Pigs Get Fat; Hogs Get Slaughtered

This was a favorite saying of a former co-worker. It was his response to employees who were always looking for ways to beat the system or get just a little bit more than whatever the rules allowed. This co-worker was responsible for managing our company's IRS audits, and through the years, he had learned a min/max axiom of how to deal with the IRS: you'll get nothing for which you do not ask, but ask for too much and they may get suspicious and dig more deeply into your tax return.

Nothing wrong with trying to get the best deal you can when you're negotiating, but know when to stop. If you get too greedy, the other party may walk out on you, and in the words of *Caddyshack's* Judge Smails, "You'll get nothing!"

Plan and Save for Retirement

I'm sure it's hard for younger people to feel the necessity for retirement savings when retirement is still decades away—especially when as a young adult you're not yet making a very nice salary and the costs of early adulthood, student loans and a new family are high. But even if it's a modest amount, develop a retirement savings habit early in life and stick with it. A modest investment of only $100 per month beginning at age 25 could easily grow to a balance of over $150,000 by the time you retire.

A consistently followed retirement savings plan will give you so many more options when you get late in your career and allow you to retire on your own terms (not when your bank account says you can).

Paul T. Morgan

What Will Your Retirement Look Like?

As a young adult, my picture of the perfect retirement was the ultimate life of leisure: play golf four days a week and go fishing the other three. Every week.

Now that I'm there, I realize the perfect retirement includes a healthy balance of leisure and service. Yes, after several decades of hard work, I want to enjoy the fun and relaxation that my career permitted too infrequently. But I've found that balancing my play time with time spent serving other people—doing something that makes a difference in others' lives—provides just as much "feel good" as my recreation. Long before you reach retirement age, plan your retirement—not just your financial planning but also your time planning.

"All work and no play makes Jack a dull boy." That old adage is true. But also true is my corollary to it: "All play and no service makes Jack a grumpy old man."

Don't Sweat the Petty Things

… and don't pet the sweaty things.

No real wisdom here—just too fun to leave this one out.

Paul T. Morgan

Find Time to Spend with Dad

This will sound selfish, but always find time to spend with me. There's an old Harry Chapin song entitled *Cat's in the Cradle* (look it up on YouTube) whose lyrics tell the story of a father who was always so busy with his own life that he missed a lot of his son's growing up years. His young son was always asking him "When you coming home, Dad?" and asking him to come play with him. But the dad always responded by saying that he was really busy today but "we'll get together soon." Of course, "soon" never came. Then his son grew up and the roles reversed with the dad asking the son to spend time together and the son being too busy with his own life to find time to go see his dad. The dad then realized that his son had grown up to be just like himself. It made him regret being too busy to spend time with his son when he was young. That song really hit home to me as a young father and inspired me to always find time for the two of you.

But although the song is about a father who was too busy for his son, it really does cut both ways. Until your own kids grow up and leave home, you'll never understand what a big deal it is to me to have you guys call me, come visit and plan events for us to enjoy together. Don't ever get too busy for your kids—that's number one. But please don't get too busy for me either.

Chapter Two
Your Relationship with Others

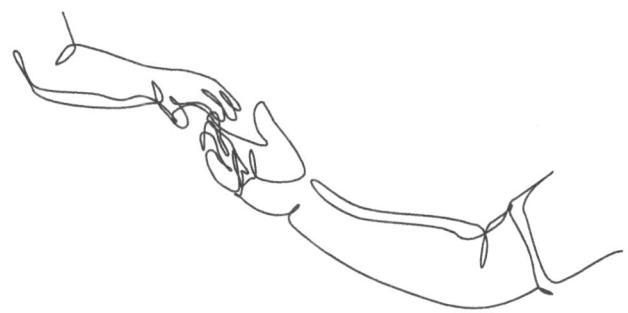

Don't Expect People to Change Who They Are

A woman falls in love with a guy who has some unattractive traits and habits, thinking that once married, he will change those traits and habits. Nope. Voters elect as president a person about whom they have some character reservations, hoping that once elected, he will "grow into the office." Nope. Coach Bill Parcells once told his team, "You are who your record says you are."

Yes, we all have the capacity to improve ourselves, and to some extent, we all can and will change for the better. But if your interest in a person is conditioned upon him or her achieving a desired change in who they are today, you would be wise to listen to the counsel of poet Maya Angelou:

"When someone shows you who they are, believe them."

It's Not About You

It's human nature. You meet someone new and you want her to like you. So to make a good impression on her, you try to think of cool things to tell her about yourself—what you like, places you've been, your hobbies, your favorite (fill in the blank). You wonder to yourself, "What can I tell her about myself that will make that good first impression?" Answer—nothing.

What will make the better impression on her would be to ask HER those same questions: "What do YOU like? Where have YOU traveled? What are YOUR hobbies?"

Showing interest in the other person first will make a far better impression than anything you can tell about your own self. And then, most likely, flattered by your selfless interest in her, she will ask the same questions of you, giving you the chance to say everything you wanted to say in the first place—only now to someone who is really interested in hearing it.

Paul T. Morgan

Allow Your Children to Fail, But Then Be There to Help Them Up

How active should a parent be in stepping in to help his or her children achieve a goal or overcome an obstacle? In my view, there are two extremes here, both to be avoided.

The "helicopter parent" who always rushes in to promote or protect his child may think he's helping his child succeed. But more likely he's preventing his child from learning to do things for himself and failing to allow him to learn how to accept and deal with disappointment.

The parent who offers no comfort or support when his child fails may think he's teaching his child to suck it up and be tough. But more likely he's making it harder for his child to recover and learn from his disappointment—and probably missing a good chance to show his child how much he loves him.

Find the right balance here. Allow your children to do things for themselves and attempt things that might appear to be unachievable. That will demonstrate your confidence in them. But when disappointments come, be there to encourage and console them—and (if asked) help them decide how to respond to their disappointment.

Praise Effort, Not Results

We all need the encouragement and self-esteem that comes from receiving praise now and then. Sometimes we need that praise more when our hard work and best efforts come up short than when we are successful. Self-esteem comes naturally when we "win" and there are plenty of people around who will tell us how great we are when we achieve something significant. Nothing wrong with congratulating a child or co-worker who achieves a goal. But look for opportunities to praise them when their effort was just as good as that of the winner but perhaps the chips just simply didn't fall their way. When you praise the *effort* instead of the *result*, you're recognizing the only part of the process over which they truly had control.

Paul T. Morgan

Praise in Public, Criticize in Private

Good advice if the point of either is to help a person grow and gain self-confidence.

Be a Barnabas

Without trying to figure out why, make a quick list of five people around whom you enjoy being. Then try to find the common traits among the five people. I'll bet you find that each of them has a knack for encouraging the people around them. Although we don't read a lot about him, one of my favorite character names in the Bible is Barnabas, whose name translates "son of encouragement."

Some people are simply no fun to be around because they just seem to dampen the mood wherever they are. It's said that everyone has the capacity to brighten a room—some people when they walk in, others when they walk out. It has to be genuine (people can see through a phony gesture) but look for people who seem to be feeling down and find a way to be their Barnabas.

Paul T. Morgan

There's More Than One Way to Skin a Cat

I have to wonder how this expression became so widely used. I mean, I don't like cats, but did we ever really skin them? But we all know what the expression means—there's more than one way to do most jobs.

Sometimes people will help you with your tasks (laundry, loading the dishwasher, trimming the shrubs). And guess what—their way probably won't match *your* way. But also guess what—their way is probably just as good. Or at least good enough.

When you're the one skinning the cat (this is just a metaphor, right?) skin him however you like to see cats skinned. But when receiving help from others, simply show gratitude for the help and don't correct the skinning method.

Be Careful with Whom You Hang Out

1 Corinthians 15:33 "Bad company corrupts good morals."

Mom and I were honored when friends and family would comment on how well our children "turned out." Their compliments suggested that this outcome was the result of good parenting. And I'd like to believe we played some role in shaping your moral character, but truth is the two of you boosted your odds of "turning out" well by choosing for yourselves friends who also possessed good moral character. James, Brandon, Zach, Anna, Maddie, Laura, Rachel, Holly—you guys all helped each other embrace what was good and supported whatever good teaching you were getting from your parents. Had you chosen friends with lesser values, it's unlikely that Mom and I could have overcome their negative influence.

But the value of surrounding yourself with "good" people didn't end when you reached adulthood. In fact, now that you are away from home and our direct influence, choosing the right people with whom to hang out is more important today than ever.

Paul T. Morgan

Widen Your Circle of Hospitality

So in the preceding section, using a Bible verse as an introduction, I encouraged you to hang out with "good" people—folks who could influence you in positive ways. But Jesus regularly dined with the folks that his culture considered to be the bad actors of society, telling his critics that those who are whole have no need for a physician, only those who are sick. So how do we square those two Biblical teachings? I'm practicing theology without a degree here, but here's my take:

Jesus carefully chose a group of twelve men to be his apostles—his inner circle of "friends" with whom he would share life and draw encouragement. But he also reached beyond his inner circle of friends to extend compassion and mercy to those marginalized by his society.

ACU professor Dr. Richard Beck has written several books on the subject of hospitality—a word he uses to define how compassionate and welcoming we are to others. Dr. Beck observes that each of us has a "circle of hospitality"—a comfort zone of people beyond our inner circle of friends to whom we are willing to show compassion and mercy. But he also observes (as did Jesus) that this circle of hospitality often seems to have a boundary that extends only wide enough to include PLU's (people like us)—people who look like us, think like us and believe like us. And we find it very uncomfortable to extend our hospitality to those on the other side of that boundary.

The story of The Good Samaritan challenges us to widen our circle of hospitality beyond our PLU's to the marginalized of our society who need our compassion the most. It's a wonderful story that should call all of us to a higher level of hospitality than what is comfortable.

Paul T. Morgan

Forgive ... But Forget?

You've heard it all your life: forgive and forget. Good advice but I'm not sure it means exactly what it says. When someone really hurts you, can you really erase from your memory that it happened? And if they do the same hurtful thing a second, third or fourth time, can you really convince your mind each time that this new occurrence is a first-time offense? I don't think so.

Our legal system has a process called deferred adjudication: a first-time offender for a traffic violation is put on a form of probation. Go 90 days without repeating the same offense, and the charges are dropped. But do it again next week and you'll be charged with BOTH offenses!

Maybe the ability to forgive and truly forget a hurtful act would be the most Christ-like response, but for us humans in our personal relationships, I'm not sure that's a realistic expectation. Maybe a more realistic expectation would be something closer to the deferred adjudication principle: if you hurt me once and you never do it again, it should be easy for me to dismiss your actions as unintentional and "let it go." But if you keep doing to me whatever it is over and over, I don't think you can expect me to simply forget it each time it happens.

Count to 10

The saying has been around for centuries: "When you're mad, count to 10 before saying anything." That advice (updated for the age of social media) is now more important than ever: When you're mad, count to 10 before you hit "send"—and if you're really mad, wait until tomorrow morning to begin counting.

Paul T. Morgan

Can There be More Than One Truth?

I used to believe that truth was absolute—facts are what they are and people either accept them or they don't. But I was a party in a mediation several years ago in which the other party and I disagreed sharply as to exactly what had happened to create the issue being mediated. I expected the mediator to sort out the facts, discern which of us was telling "the truth" and ask the other to accept it.

But the mediator (probably knowing there was no way she could truly discern the historical facts) asked each of us to accept that the other was recalling the past precisely - at least as precisely as he or she remembered it. To each of us, our own version of the story was spot-on accurate. Neither of us was trying to distort the facts or deceive anyone—we simply each held a different "truth."

There will be times when a disagreement will need to be resolved without either party being granted the satisfaction of being deemed as "right" and neither forced into insincerely admitting to being "wrong."

Don't Bluff

Sometimes you'll be tempted to issue a threat or warning to someone whose behavior you're trying to influence. We see it all the time with parents who tell their kids, "If you don't stop (fill in the blank) I'm going to (fill in the blank)." But the threat is hollow because they never really intend to follow through on it—they are simply hoping the threat will get the desired outcome. But what happens when the one who is threatened calls the bluff? Now the one who issued the warning must either carry through with an action they really don't want to take or be exposed as a bluffer. And if you're bluffing, that destroys the credibility of any future threats because the other person knows now that you don't really mean it.

Think before you issue the warning, "Am I really willing to make good on this threat?" If so, go ahead and issue the warning and then be willing to live with the consequences of following through.

But in some instances, a better approach, I think, is to simply tell the offender, "If you don't (fill in the blank), you're going to force me to make a really difficult decision that *might* include (fill in the blank) and neither of us will like it if I choose the tougher of my options." Of course, if you never really exercise the tougher option, this warning will also ring hollow. But it gives you some wiggle room to back out later without impugning your credibility ... and leaves the one threatened to wonder what if.

Paul T. Morgan

The Power of the Handwritten Note

In an era of electronic everything and social media, it's so easy and efficient to use email and text messaging to communicate with others. And there's nothing wrong with using those efficiencies to make our lives simpler and easier. But sometimes when you want to make an impression on someone or let them know you *really* mean whatever it is you're wanting to say, use the old-fashioned handwritten note. Because so few people seem to take the time to do this anymore, you'll be surprised how big an impression it will make on the receiver when they realize how much thought and effort you put into it.

Be Kind to Old People

They can be frustrating. They're the ones who slow you down when you get stuck behind them on the freeway or in the check-out line at the grocery store. They are sometimes very unfiltered—they will tell you exactly what they think and not choose their words very carefully. But the older I get and the more time I spend in volunteer service to seniors at care centers, the more I understand their perspective and the more compassion I have for their place in our society. Imagine no longer feeling as strong and healthy as you used to feel. Imagine no longer having the self-esteem enriching position of control and responsibility you held in your career. Imagine having younger people (who lack your years of wisdom) being in charge and making all the rules for society—or for you personally.

I am so looking forward to my golden years and the opportunity to enjoy more leisure time. But I am fearful of how it will feel to gradually become less and less relevant in the world. I fear becoming lonely and isolated. But I think I would feel much less lonely or isolated if the younger members of my world noticed me, sought my opinion on important issues and simply showed kindness and appreciation for the role I played in creating the world they now enjoy.

Paul T. Morgan

Park at the Far End of the Parking Lot

Help me understand this: a young, health-conscious person goes to the gym and works out for an hour to improve cardiovascular health … and then backs up traffic in the grocery store parking lot waiting for a car to back out of a parking space right next to the door. Really?

Make it a habit to park at the far end of the parking lot and leave the convenient up-close spaces for older folks and mothers with young children. The extra distance won't add 30 seconds to your errand time, you'll get a little bit of exercise … and you'll get fewer dings in your car doors.

Tip Generously

Working as a waiter or waitress is a much harder job than it appears. It pays very little, they must tolerate lots of inconsiderate and ungrateful customers and the people who do these jobs are frequently working more than one job to help their families. A couple of extra dollars will help them more than it will hurt you. And you'll add a little joy to someone working a job where they rarely receive the appreciation they deserve.

Paul T. Morgan

It's Only Funny if EVERYONE Laughs

A good sense of humor can lighten the mood in many situations. You both know I love to joke. But we have to be careful when telling jokes that we don't offend folks who don't find our humor so funny. Notice I say "we" here because I've had my share of moments when I was not as careful and sensitive as I should have been.

Most jokes and "dig" comments play on one of two themes: a derogatory dig at the expense of someone else or a play on some kind of stereotype (e.g. Aggie and lawyer jokes). When done in jest and with people who are not overly sensitive, they can be fun for everyone around. Most people know when a joke or clever comment is good-natured and they will laugh along with you—even if the joke is at their own expense. And if you're going to take a shot at others, you'd better be a good enough sport to take it when the dig is at *your* expense. But sometimes the dig hits a little too close to home for some people or they don't understand that the joke or comment was intended in jest. This can create some awkward moments or really hurt some feelings.

My advice here (and much of this I have learned the hard way): (1) Make sure you know your audience. If there's someone present you don't know very well, don't assume they'll accept it well. (2) Avoid jokes that have a racial, ethnic or gender-based undertone—a pretty good chance you'll hit a nerve with one of those topics (remember Mom's advice. "Don't say anything ethnic!") (3) Avoid subjects about which you know someone present to be particularly sensitive. Best overall rule of thumb here: It's only funny if *everyone* laughs. If someone's not laughing, it's not funny, it's hurtful.

Paul T. Morgan

Don't Be the "One-up" Guy

Have you ever been around the guy who has to always "one-up" everyone else at the table? Someone tells a funny story—he has to tell a funnier story. You met someone famous—he's met someone even more famous. You made a hole-in-one—he made a hole-in-*zero*.

No matter the subject, whatever wonderful or funny thing someone tells, he has something even more wonderful and funnier. That guy has not lived a more spectacular life than anyone else at the table—he just has such low self-esteem that he needs to hear himself say out loud how wonderful he is. And sadly, he thinks it makes everyone else think he's wonderful. But guess what? That's not what they think.

Don't be the "one-up" guy.

Don't be a Mooch

I bet you've both seen lots of folks who seem to always be "taking" and rarely "giving." They are always asking for a free ticket to a game or to borrow a tool or for someone to do a favor for them. But they never seem to have a free ticket, tool or favor for anyone else. Don't be a mooch. Accept a kindness when it's offered, but don't be "that guy" who's always standing there with his hand out.

Paul T. Morgan

Stewardship / Charity

Whether you're earning a lot of money or a very modest amount, set aside a percentage of what you earn to give to others. I don't recall how we determined the amount, but several years ago, Mom and I decided to give 8% of our earnings (before taxes) to others. In good times and tough times, we always set aside that percentage to give to others. There's nothing magical about 8%. You decide what percentage works for you, but whatever you decide, give it consistently—even in years when you may be facing financial challenges.

So, who are the "others" to whom we should give? A lot of preachers will suggest that nearly all of your stewardship offering should be given to the church. And they will use Paul's instructions to the Christians in Corinth as the basis for that rule. But in Matthew Chapter 25, Jesus paints a picture of the Judgment Day. The people Jesus commends in that parable weren't giving to the church—they were giving directly to the people who needed something (a cup of water, food, clothing, etc.). Certainly, if you're going to be a member of a church, you need to financially support that church and its ministries. But set aside some of your charitable giving for other organizations that need our support. And set aside some money to give directly to people in need—friends, family members or even strangers. When you see these people hurting and needing a helping hand, don't wait for the church or some other organization to help them—do it yourself. You'll be surprised how good it feels to help someone directly out of your own pocket.

What Would Dad Do?

Service

Get involved in one or more of the ministries of your church, but find your own personal service project or mission to help other people. That special service project doesn't necessarily have to be connected to your church's ministries. But it does need to be something for which you have a passion, or else it will be hard to regularly commit time and energy to it for a long period of time.

After Mom died, I wanted so badly to find something really big and significant I could do for others that would honor her. I wanted to find something that would raise a ton of money or help thousands of people. So, for a long time, I didn't really do anything because I couldn't think of anything really big or significant. Then I read a story that helped me see things from a different perspective:

One day a man was walking along the seashore and he noticed thousands of starfish that had washed up on the beach during the high tide. He then saw a young boy who was picking up starfish and tossing them back into the ocean. He asked the boy what he was doing. The boy replied, "These starfish will die if they don't get back into the water, so I'm saving them." The man laughed and said, "Young man, there are thousands of starfish scattered along miles of this beach. Do you really think you're going to make that much of a difference?" The

Paul T. Morgan

boy looked down at the starfish in his hand and replied, "Well, I can make a difference for *this* one." And he tossed it back into the ocean.

You don't have to save *all* of the starfish to make a difference for some of them. Find your personal area of service, help the people you can help and don't worry about how big or significant it is.

Random Acts of Kindness

It's important to plan acts of service to other people—intentional acts of charity or kindness. But every day you will encounter someone who could use a little boost. The concept of "random acts of kindness" suggests that you don't *plan* to do something nice for someone—you just react to the situation when it shows up in front of you. And random acts of kindness aren't big things—they are usually just an act of thoughtfulness that cost you very little: let someone in front of you in traffic or the grocery store line; pay for the order of the customer in line behind you in the drive-through; write a note of encouragement to a co-worker who's having a bad week. You'll be surprised how wonderful it makes both of you feel.

Paul T. Morgan

Serve Anonymously When Possible

When you make a charitable gift or perform an act of service for someone, when possible, do it anonymously. Although the person being served probably gets the same benefit whether or not you get the "credit" for the act, your motive will never be questioned (either by yourself or others) if your gift or act of service is done without fanfare. Some benefactors seem to enjoy making their gifts very public—frequently in a manner that seeks attention from the media. Although their gifts may be very generous, it makes one wonder whether the motivation behind the gift or act was wholesome or with the intent of attracting "look at me" praise and attention for the donor. Do it anonymously and the only praise you'll receive will come from God. And that should be enough.

Courtesy

Treat others better than they expect and deserve. Seek out opportunities to surprise people with kindness. Say "thank you" often. Open doors for others. Be outgoing and friendly with wait staff at restaurants—they appreciate this more than you think they do.

Paul T. Morgan

Tolerance

It's important that you hold true to your values and principles. But holding *yourself* to those values doesn't mean you should hold *others* to those same values. This can be a tough rule to follow when you're sure that your position on an issue is "right" or God's will for us. So long as their values do not infringe on your own rights or keep you from holding your values for yourself, others must be given the freedom to follow their own hearts or consciences.

You will encounter challenges to your tolerance most often on issues of faith, politics or social issues. Just as your particular view on an issue seems so clearly "right" to you, it's likely that the person with the opposing view is just as sincere in his belief as you are in yours. The best example I can give for this principle is the issue of prayer in school.

Living where we do in the "Bible Belt" we frequently hear Christians argue in favor of allowing public prayers in school or at school functions such as graduation or sporting events. Since many Christians consider their faith to be the only true faith, they feel obligated to "stand up" for their faith by insisting on preserving the practice of Christian-based prayers at school events or displaying the Ten Commandments on school property. But consider the perspective of those who do not embrace Christianity. Imagine if you lived in a community where Islam or Judaism was the prevailing faith and their followers insisted on asking your children to listen to their prayers or see the Koran displayed on the walls at their school. You would be greatly offended.

There's a fine line between tolerating an opposing view and condoning it. When I allow my fellow man to hold a position with which I strongly disagree or support a social practice that I consider to be "wrong," I'm not condoning their view or failing to "stand up" for my own belief. I'm simply following the principle that says that if I want others to be tolerant of me, I must show tolerance to them.

Paul T. Morgan

Love Does

I don't read very many books, but one of the few I have read in the past few years is *Love Does* by Bob Goff (a book Meredith gave me to read). Goff's message is the same message Jesus taught in Matthew Chapter 25. True love is not about simply feeling compassion for people who find themselves in need—true love *acts* on that compassion and meets their needs with food, clothing, money and companionship. Love doesn't just feel—it *does*.

Chapter Three
That's Life

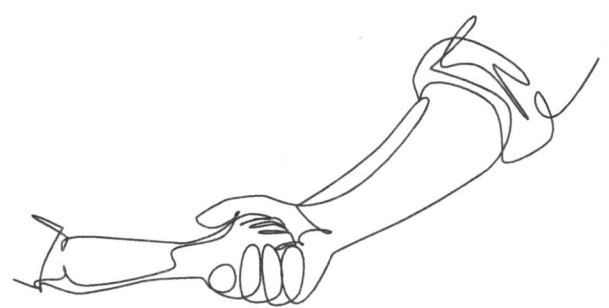

Life is Not Fair

When you were young kids, I bet you got tired of hearing my Big Tex anecdote about life not being fair. But it's the truth. If you define "fair" as getting what you deserve, life is not fair. Sometimes you'll get better than you deserve and sometimes you'll get a lot worse. You will remember the "worse" times more quickly than the "better" ones, but for most people there will be plenty of both during their lifetimes.

Two points here: (1) When something really good happens for you, make a point to recall that good break the next time something goes wrong; and (2) Be prepared for the times when the fairness breaks go against you. You may not be able to anticipate what bad break you'll get, but you can accept in advance that some kind of bad break will come someday and be mentally prepared to deal with it.

Fair Does Not Mean Equal

Lots of parents try really hard to treat their kids "equally." If they give something of value to one child, they feel they have to give something of equal value to their other children. If they spend a certain amount of money on clothing (or whatever) for one child, they must spend an equal amount of money on the other. If they spend four hours at one child's event, four hours must be spent with the other in order to be "fair."

Obviously, parents should not show favoritism among their children. But fairness does not require that children be treated equally. Your children will not all be alike. They will not be "equal." Each child is unique with specific talents, opportunities, challenges - and needs. And because their needs will be different, parents should respond to their needs differently. A child who is not as gifted or healthy as her siblings may require more help from her parents. One child may encounter more bad breaks than another and need more attention at times than the sibling on whom the sun seems to shine more often.

When life treats your children unequally (and it will) don't be reluctant to respond in unequal measures. And if one of your children questions whether you're being "fair," explain to them that as a parent, "fair" means doing everything you can to offset the effects of the fact that life is *not* fair.

Paul T. Morgan

No Whining

Remember Eeyore from *Winnie the Pooh*? Everywhere he went he had a gray cloud hovering above him. He lived in a perpetual self-pity party. When bad breaks come your way, there's a natural temptation to complain. I'm not sure why—I guess we want others to sympathize with our plight. Or maybe we want to play the martyr and be praised for withstanding tough times. But my experience has been that complaining about your circumstances rarely earns you any more sympathy or compassion than you'd get by simply sucking it up, accepting your circumstances and making the best of them. Everyone loves a winner. No one loves a whiner. Don't be an Eeyore.

Cut Down the Tree

One day not long after the end of the Civil War, a woman in the South took General Robert E. Lee to see the burned-out remains of what had once been a beautiful old tree standing in her front yard. The woman loved the tree and General Lee listened patiently as she cried and cursed the Yankees whose artillery fire had destroyed the tree's limbs and much of its trunk. When the woman finished her rage, she looked at General Lee, waiting for some denunciation of the Yankees, or at least a word of sympathy. But Lee paused for a moment, and simply said to the woman: "Cut it down, my dear madam, and forget it."

Holding a grudge will never right a wrong. It will only keep the grudge-holder from moving on and enjoying life.

Paul T. Morgan

Why Do Only the Very Young and Very Old Get to Say Whatever They Want?

Toddlers will say whatever comes to their minds—completely oblivious to how inappropriate or insensitive it might be. But no one seems to get offended—we just all understand that they are too young to know any better. Similarly, the very old are frequently unfiltered—and we all just laugh it off as something old people do.

No advice or wisdom to share here—just an observation I find amusing.

Chapter Four
How Our World Works

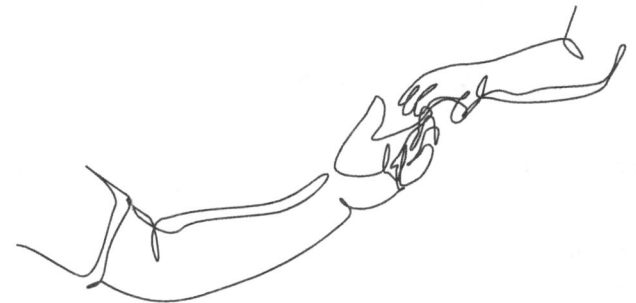

Insurance

In its simplest terms, insurance is a tool that allows people to pool and share their individual risks—a risk defined as an event that would have an adverse financial effect on the victim of the event. The concepts of insurance are pretty simple: (1) Sooner or later bad things will happen to everyone, but probably not all at the same time, and (2) If you'll help me cover the cost of bad things when they happen to me, I'll help you cover the cost when bad things happen to you.

An insurance policy is essentially an agreement among a group of at-risk people to share their risks and associated costs with the insurance company serving as the middleman to spread the costs around among the members of the group. The premiums we pay represent our share of the cost of bad things happening to everyone else in our group.

Some people look at the premiums they paid in years when they had no claims and think, "Man, that was a bad investment—I paid out all that money and got nothing in return!" Not true—what you "got" was the peace of mind and protection that you would have had help paying your expenses *if* something bad had happened. That's not "nothing."

The other misconception some people have about insurance is that if they have insurance, they should incur absolutely no out-of-pocket cost if the bad thing happens to them. Insurance policies require the policyholder to pay some portion of the cost of the bad thing (called a deductible) to make sure the policyholder has some "skin in the game." What incentive do you have to be careful if there is absolutely no cost to you if your carelessness is what causes the bad thing to happen?

So, what risks should I insure and when? Here are my strategies on the various types of insurance available:

Life insurance:
If you're single and have no one dependent on your earnings, life insurance is a bad buy—you're covering a risk that doesn't really exist. But if you have family members dependent upon your earnings (especially young children) this is a risk worth covering with insurance.

Health insurance:
This is a must-have. Sooner or later you will sustain a really serious injury or illness. Without insurance, you could be stuck with a huge hospital and doctor bill (could be hundreds of thousands of dollars). Trying to cover this risk on your own could devastate your savings and put you into huge debt.

Auto and homeowner's insurance:
Just like health insurance, the risk here of a really huge loss is too great a risk to bear alone. Buy policies with deductibles as high as you can stand (this will reduce the amount of your premium) but don't try to go it alone.

Paul T. Morgan

Long-term care insurance:
Without this insurance, Mom's care during her long illness would have been devastating to our family's savings. The cost of 24/7 care for a long period of time can be huge. The risk here is not so great when you're still young, but by the time you get into your 40's, buy it. If you wait until you need it, the insurance companies won't sell it to you.

Disability insurance:
This coverage replaces a portion of your salary if you get sick or hurt and can't perform your job for a long period of time. This is a very real risk, and if purchased through your employer, the premiums are pretty reasonable. Buy it.

Get Your Legal Stuff in Order

Probably the best contingency planning advice ever is, "Always wear clean underwear just in case you're in an accident." But a close second is to get your legal affairs in order.

Without a will, the state's laws (or perhaps a court) will decide what happens to your assets when you die. Those rulings might or might not reflect your intentions. Even if your earthly possessions are modest and you have a very simple family structure, create a will and then update it anytime there is a significant change in your situation.

But a will controls only what happens when you die. So many of life's contingencies are created by some kind of incapacitation while you're alive. I won't go into the details here but there are a number of legal documents that could become very important to your care if you became incapacitated: durable power of attorney, healthcare power of attorney, living will, etc. Two important points here: (1) As important as *what* these documents advise is *who* they appoint to make decisions for you if you are no longer able to make those decisions yourself, and (2) Once incapacitated, you will no longer be able to make these choices. And like a will, in the absence of specific directions from you, a court may be forced to make these decisions for you.

Paul T. Morgan

There are lots of self-help legal document services available on the internet, and those are better than doing nothing. But I recommend that you spend the extra money to have them done right by an attorney—someone you know and trust (like your cousin David Allen).

What Makes Us Smart Can Also Make Us Ignorant

One definition of "intelligence" is the capacity to learn. I heard a speaker once who explained that the one quality that distinguishes advanced animals from those less advanced is pattern recognition—the ability to learn from previous experiences: "I've seen this situation before, I remember what happened then and so, I know how to respond to it this time." (Once you get burned by a hot stove you learn not to touch it again.) Humans, according to this theory, are the most intelligent of all animals because our brains have the greatest capacity to store and quickly recall patterns they have seen before.

But there's another edge to this sword. That which makes us more intelligent can actually work against us. Two examples:

We can become so skilled at pattern recognition that we sometimes draw conclusions based upon what we believe to be a pattern we've seen before—when in fact, the current situation is really nothing at all like the previous experience upon which we are drawing our conclusion. You can make the argument that this thought process is the premise upon which all prejudice is based. It can cause us unknowingly to paint people with a very broad brush. Someone has a bad experience with a person from a different race or ethnic background and they presume that all members of those groups possess the same negative qualities. You meet a member of a particular faith

Paul T. Morgan

background, learn what he believes about certain faith issues and assume all members of that faith group hold those same beliefs. Jumping to conclusions like this doesn't show your intelligence—it demonstrates blind ignorance.

Secondly, our "gift" of pattern recognition can lead us down the same old road as previous experiences and stymie the creativity that breeds innovation. If your mind is trained to assume that the proper response to a particular experience will serve you well each time that experience is presented, you'll never learn to "think outside the box" and try new solutions. All significant inventions and discoveries resulted from someone who was unwilling to accept the same old answer they had always accepted. As a society, rigid pattern-recognition thinking will stymie the creativity we need to find cures for diseases and solve other social and economic problems.

The lesson here is two-fold and seemingly a mutual contradiction: You need the capacity to both learn and *un*-learn. Learn from your mistakes and keep your hand off the hot stove. But don't be so quick to recognize patterns when forming opinions about the character of other people or looking for solutions to problems.

Vote

It's easy to become so jaded by the antics of politicians (and their supporters) that sometimes you just want to check out and sit out the whole election process. That won't fix the system. Become informed and vote. Even if your candidate has little chance of winning (or is almost guaranteed of winning), make your voice count.

Paul T. Morgan

For Most People, "Right" Means What's Right for *Me*

Listen to any public figure, co-worker or family member espouse their opinions on almost any social or political issue, and I'll bet you find that their position on the issue is controlled by what's in it for them. We'd all like to think that we are wise and altruistic enough to discern the "right" answer on any question without allowing our own personal self-interests to influence our decision. My observation through the years suggests otherwise. Examples:

Wealthy people tend to favor lower taxes and limited government entitlements to the not-so-fortunate (leaving more money in their own pockets) while the not-so-fortunate nearly unanimously favor a higher tax burden on the wealthy to fund government assistance that would level the playing field for themselves. Coincidence? I think not.

Lots of Christians hold very strong pro-life opinions. But watch how their positions change when it's their own teenage daughter who gets pregnant.

Listen to all the auto workers complain about unfair competition from overseas automakers and clamor for tariffs to protect their jobs here in America. Then watch those same auto workers go to Wal-Mart and purchase inexpensive clothing made with cheap labor in China or Vietnam.

The lesson here: No matter how sincere and unselfish we think we are, it is simply very difficult to set aside our own personal perspective, view the world through the lens of the other person and choose a position on any issue that is not in our own self-interests. (Remember the movie *Trading Places* with Eddie Murphy and Dan Aykroyd? Both the businessman and the beggar saw the world very differently after their stations in life were switched). So, when you have a disagreement with someone over some moral issue or principle, just remember that *neither* of you is as objective as you think you are.

Paul T. Morgan

The Risk of Wealth Inequality

However you measure it, wealth inequality in America is real. There is a huge (and increasing) gap in wealth between the top and bottom 20% of our country's population. This disparity in wealth (and therefore in standard of living) increases the natural tension between the haves and have-nots in our society. That's easy to see. What's not so easy is what to do about it.

There are two extreme views on how active the government should be in distributing (or redistributing) wealth among its citizens: (1) A very *limited* role from the government that allows our free-market system (i.e. capitalism) to distribute wealth among the citizens based upon each citizen's individual contribution to the country's economy, and (2) A very *active* role from the government that attempts to "level the playing field" among citizens by offsetting the inequities caused by the disparity in intelligence, creativity, physical health and opportunity among the citizens.

The government essentially has two tools at its disposal for the purpose of distributing / redistributing wealth: (1) laws which place restrictions on what its citizens are allowed to do, and (2) taxes, which are used to take money from the more prosperous citizens and redistribute it to the less prosperous citizens.

During my lifetime, I've seen the government become more and more active in the process of wealth redistribution: increasing taxes on the citizens who are doing well and using those tax revenues to increase government-funded benefits to the citizens who aren't doing as well. It's been a move further and further away from pure "capitalism"—but critics who call it "socialism" are exaggerating.

In my view, our nation (and its people) would benefit best (short- and long-term) from a system that borrows from both of these idealistic models: a system that maintains the personal economic incentives and rewards for innovation and hard work but also provides a compassionate helping hand to those who, through no fault of their own, are disadvantaged. This sounds simple and logical enough, right?

But unfortunately, with each passing year, we seem to elect leaders who hold one extreme view or the other. There appear to be fewer and fewer leaders (or citizens) willing to compromise somewhere in the middle.

My fear is that the widening chasm between the folks holding these two ideologies will create an increasingly polarized population—exacerbating the divisive "us against them" social tension in our country.

My generation should apologize to yours for the social tension we've created. My wish for you and your kids is that your generation will find it easier to find common ground on these issues and put the "United" back in the United States of America.

Paul T. Morgan

Chapter Five

Wrap-up

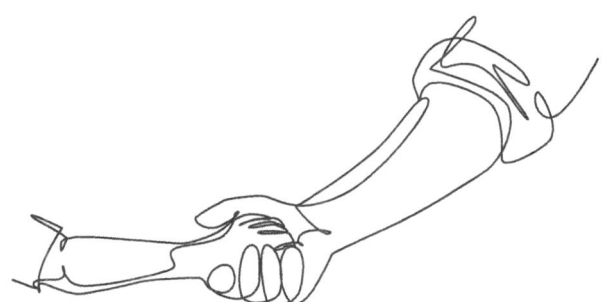

What Would Jesus Do?

Obviously, my title here *What Would Dad Do?* was borrowed from the WWJD bracelets popularized in the 1990's. And looking back over most of my entries here, nearly all of them are simply specific examples of the broader principle of asking, "What Would Jesus Do?" And it should go without saying, but in every situation you find yourself, if you ask and answer *that* question properly, you won't need to wonder what Dad would do ☺

www.ingramcontent.com/pod-product-compliance
Lightning Source LLC
Chambersburg PA
CBHW031452040426
42444CB00007B/1066